ONE

ONE can make a difference

By

Trish Wilson

Cover designed by Trish Wilson
Cover graphics enhanced by Yoli Thompson

Names, characters, places, and incidents are from the author's personal experience. Names of people have been changed to protect the personal information of said individuals.

Printed in the United States of America

First Printing: December 2018
Trish Wilson

ISBN: 9781729046623

You have been given
ONE more day to do
ONE more thing to change
ONE more life even if it is your own.
Don't miss the opportunity.

—TRISH WILSON

For MOM
who did more than one thing daily
to change my life from the very beginning.

CONTENTS

Trish Wilson

A NOTE FROM THE AUTHOR

There is nothing in a new writer's mind scarier than a blank page. A white sheet staring at you and wondering what will be placed upon it. But in starting the adventure of writing, I don't see this page as a monster trying to overwhelm my mind and spirit, but as a blank canvas waiting for the first brush strokes of a masterpiece. I am excited to share this new adventure with you and pray that the pages speak to your heart as you read. Remember that each of us is given the opportunity in our days on earth to live each day as it was intended, as a new possibility, a chance to meet someone we have never met before, a lesson in growth of who we are as individuals, a stretch of our abilities or improvement of our inabilities, and ONE more day to do ONE more thing to change ONE more life, even if it is our own. Blessings!

Trish Wilson

INTRODUCTION

I am a firm believer that you aren't where you are in life by chance. Sure, you made choices that led you where you are – but how did you choose? Did you ever wonder what your life would have been like if you had taken the other option? Or choice? I do that on occasion, but the incredible thing is that as I look back, I see the choices that I made, both good and bad have brought me to the path where I am today.

Within our lives there have been many paths we have chosen to take. Some were pleasant with beautiful scenery and interesting people, who walked beside us or caught up to us and shared the road for a spell. Some paths have been lonely, perhaps dark and lonely ones we could not wait to end or lead to a brighter path. But regardless of the path, those who were traveling with us, beside us or perhaps their path just seemed to cross ours for a split second, seemed to make a difference.

Those were not just chance meetings, pleasant coincidences or personal orchestrations. They were divine appointments. Moments in time that were designed by the hand of God, long before we knew those people. Perfect meetings that would take place at just the right spot in time in our lives to teach us, to comfort us, to bless us and all the while help us as we traveled along our path. These lives made our lives better – stronger – and our relationships more than just casual happenings. Our lives drew from their life and in the end, we are better for it.

Others, who seem to make our path rockier or darker, harder somehow, in turn give us a moment to lean on God, seek His solutions, ask and gain His strength, comfort and endurance. Though at the time, we could not see the good in meeting that person or even having them in our lives, God used them to draw us closer to Him and to develop a new character trait that provided for the journey ahead. Difficulties are opportunities in disguise. The only difference in either is our reaction to them.

In sharing, how each of our lives affects the lives of those around us, I realized that sharing some of the people who impacted my life in the past 10 years would make that point. During these years I have had the privilege of working with children with physical disabilities, type 1 diabetes, Down syndrome and cancer at Texas Lions Camp in Kerrville, Texas, and have been able to spend time with some very incredible people. Don't get me wrong, none of these individuals are famous, at least not to the rest of the world, but they are to me. They haven't written books, made movies, performed to huge concert halls filled with adoring fans. No, they are just extraordinary every-day people, whose paths just happened to cross mine. Their life intertwined with mine for a brief time in the past decade of my life, and I was never the same afterwards. They each taught me a principle in life that made a difference. Each of them, without knowing, brought something into my life that wasn't there before, or if it was, it was hidden, not tapped into, not recognized. I will forever remember how they touched my life, and their story will always be a part of my story.

Trish Wilson

CHAPTER 1 – BEING DIFFERENT

Jay walked onto campus worried. Worried what others would think and if he'd fit in. He had a lot going for him – athletic build, great smile and friendly personality. But concern overshadowed the positives.

When I met this good looking, young man and saw immediately he had a few reservations in the furrow of his brow, I simply tapped him on the shoulder and introduced myself. I asked him if he was excited about camp and being able to do so many activities, and he just smiled and said, "I guess so."

"Why the hesitation?" I asked.

"Not sure that I'll fit in. I'm different," he replied.

I studied Jay for a moment, smiled and said, "Well, I don't know if you noticed or not, but everybody here is different. Each of these young people has something that they are dealing with." He looked around and shrugged.

I began again, "What you put into camp is what you'll get out of camp." He smiled and looked me in the eye. I continued, "If you jump in with both feet, you'll really enjoy your time here. There's nothing you won't be able to do, if you just give yourself a chance to try. You will have a blast."

That statement made him smile. His demeanor changed, and his brow lost its wrinkles of concern. He looked at me and simply replied, "Okay, I'll try."

I walked Jay to his cabin, and on our way, he told me about his family and school. Being a teenage boy, he talked a lot about sports (soccer primarily) and, of course, girls. As we approached his cabin, one of his counselors came from the cabin running towards us. This young servant had a puzzling look on his face as if trying to multiply a multi-digit number by twelve. As he got closer, he soon had a huge smile, and I knew he had figured out the solution he was searching for. This counselor loved to high-five everyone that he met, but especially his campers. As he approached me and my young new friend, he realized that Jay had no shoulders, arms or hands on either side of his body. So, he was going to have to find another way to high-five and greet him. As he approached, and I saw that he had reached his solution, he slid into a position right in front of the young man and kicked off his shoe, stuck out his foot as if it were a hand, and simply said, "Hey there, welcome, glad to meet you."

Jay smiled, kicked off his shoe, and shook feet with his new best friend. With the counselor's arm around the young man, they walked off chatting about the fun that was in store in the week ahead. As they approached their new home for the week, Jay met and shook feet with the other campers that would soon become his family of brothers whom he would hold dear from that day forward. It was amazing to watch how one person's struggle was eased by the simple reaction of love from another.

All week, I checked in on Jay to see how he was doing and if his "being different" was making a difference in his experience. I found him at the archery range, and I knew this could be a pivotal moment not only in his week, but also his life. As the instructor went over the rules and directions for the activity, all the campers listened and watched. When the instructor asked for a volunteer, a single foot reached for the sky, along with hands from everyone else. The foot was chosen, and my young friend walked to the line. The instructor looking at the camper with no shoulders, no arms and no hands asked simply, "Do you have a plan on how you want to do this?"

A child-sized plastic chair, one you would find in any kindergarten class, was brought out and placed at the line. The young man sat down and removed his socks and shoes with his toes. The instructor knelt beside Jay and held the bow. The arrow was affixed to the bow, and the instructor waited for the instructions from the young archer. He placed the instructor where he needed him to be with verbal commands and slight touches with his feet. The instructor stretched out his arm and held the bow firmly.

Then the incredible happened. This young archer reached up with his toes and pulled back on the string holding the arrow and with minor adjustments, let loose and sent the arrow straight to target's bull's-eye. Cheers erupted from all who witnessed it. Four more times an arrow flew, and out of all the arrows, four of the five found their way to the victorious bull's-eye.

Jay smiled as he kicked his shoes back to the bench where he had once sat, allowing another one of his bunkmates to take their turn at the target. He stopped at the "Bull's-Eye Club" sign to place his signature on it with his foot. As he approached his seat, another camper asked if he could help him put on his socks and shoes. They talked about his dynamic feat and how cool it was to see him use his feet to shoot an arrow. He spent the rest of his time in the activity helping others – with hands – to hit the bull's-eye as well.

Late in the week, I found Jay in the pool leaning against the side twirling sunglasses by the earpiece between his toes. He was having a conversation with two lovely female campers. His smile spoke volumes. I just nodded his direction, and he met my nod with a huge smile and mouthed, "I like it here." He had found his niche. He wasn't concerned about being different anymore.

At the awards ceremony at the end of the week, the highest award given is for exhibiting the "CAN DO" spirit. Jay received this award. Not only for what he did himself, but for the fact that he invested time and effort in others around him, trying to help them see that they could do things they never thought possible. He was more than surprised. He thought others deserved it more than he did. I explained to him that his "CAN DO" spirit was the reason that he received it. He had jumped into this experience with both feet. He gave it all he had and encouraged others to do the same.

The things which make us different, those things we probably see as flaws, are what make us unique. Those are the very things that we bring to the table that no one else can. If we can see our differences, our flaws, our quirks as assets, we can do so much more than we could ever imagine. Because Jay lacked shoulders, arms and hands, he was forced to do things differently – to see obstacles from a different perspective. No matter what I am faced with in life, what I utilize to meet the challenge head on is within me. I have what I need in order to do what needs to be done. I must only choose to do it – to jump in with BOTH FEET and use my differences to make a difference.

Trish Wilson

CHAPTER 2 - WORTH A THOUSAND WORDS

Very seldom do you have a moment in life that makes more of an impact as one that is based on the innocence of a simple smile. Meeting Kay was such an occasion because Kay is limited in her ability to communicate. There are no letters or words made, no sentences or paragraphs uttered, no stories told. Just simple smiles when she is happy, approving or excited, and a slight frown and tears when things aren't so wonderful. Most of the time, pretty much 99.9 percent of the time, a smile dances on the lips of this young woman whose life is spent in a wheelchair. Her body has limitations, but her facial expressions are limitless.

When presented with a new challenge, her face is set in a determined clinched jaw smirk, as if telling herself and those viewing her, "I got this, just have to figure out my plan." Her inabilities are not something that tend to hinder her. Others step in and become the arms and hands that don't seem to work just right and even became her legs to move her from one spot to another. She adapts with the help of those around her to meet whatever obstacles lie in her path.

When watching Kay as she approached a horse, her smile grew larger as she grew closer. She reached out to stroke the nose of her new four-legged friend. Her wheelchair was moved to a ramp that aided her mounting, and as activity leaders and counselors moved her fragile body onto the saddle, Kay grunted and uttered noises as if she was guiding her friends in their movements. She could do very little herself to manipulate the situation, but she gave her best grunts to support those who were doing what they could.

Once straddling the high vaulted animal and supported on each side by walkers and those who would attend to her as she rode, Kay began her adventure of horseback riding for the morning. With each step, her noble companion took strides that she never could on her own feet. Her smile grew large, and squeals of delight erupted as Kay passed by trees filled with birds, as the sun danced upon her face, and as the wind fluttered her hair underneath her helmet. She couldn't speak the words, but the smile and squeals spoke volumes.

Later in the day, she had a moment of pure freedom - the freedom of limitless movement. Kay has a body that is always heavy, weighed down by limbs that are difficult to move at best. Her control of her body is anything but voluntary. She depends constantly on the help and support of others, never able to go wherever she wants, whenever she wants – a prisoner in her own skin.   But in a swimming pool, the weightlessness brings freedom, pure freedom.

With the help of those around her, Kay is slowly eased into a pool of water. The further she goes in, the more the buoyancy lifts her weighted body and allows her to move freely.   Her counselors attend to her, keeping her head upright and the floatation devices around her exactly where they need to be for her safety. She again smiles a huge face–altering smile. You can't look at her and not smile as well.   Her smiles are contagious.   She tilted her head back and allowed the sun to engulf her face. She laid her head back on the shoulder of her caretaker and allowed her to spin her around in a circle. A ballet of freedom, of ease, of sheer delight. Her joy was apparent, her limitations forgotten, and her smile unforgettable.

Nothing in our life is bad enough that a smile cannot be our companion. When we have those bad days, a smile reminds us of the good days that we have had and will have again. When we have a day filled with grief, a smile in remembrance of those that we have lost and the joy that they brought to our lives is our comfort. When we endure a day of pain, a simple smile can bring us the ray of hope that we need to see the good that can come from the pain and the truth that there is light on the other side. No matter what we are going through, there are others who need our smile to be a light in their darkness, to help them through onto the other side. Kay takes each moment and sees the positive in it. She has so much that she could be sad, angry or upset about, but her smile won't let her. Her smile is constant and so natural that not to smile is somewhat painful. There is no need for words to express how she feels; her smile says enough. I pray that my smile becomes such a permanent fixture in my days that not to smile feels unnatural. And when you need it most, I pray that my SMILE is shining bright for you to see and it encourages you.

CHAPTER 3 - A MAN OF VISION

Have you ever met someone and wondered, "Is this the real person? Or are they just putting on a front?" We walk by people all the time and say, "How are you?" and then continue without waiting for their response. Do we really care? Or are we afraid to get to know them because in turn they might know the real us?

I met a young man one day who did just that. He stopped and got to know me, the real me, before I ever knew what he was doing. Our first meeting was like any other, shaking of hands and pleasantries, followed by a myriad of questions almost interrogation style, but wait I've gotten ahead of myself.

The day I met Brian, he was being led by another person across an open field of grass. I was driving a golf cart and stopped to say hello and introduce myself. Noticing that this young man was sight impaired, I placed my hand in his hand to shake it while saying, "Hello, I'm happy to meet you." He asked me my name and told me his, as he shook my hand. Brian, wearing lightly shaded glasses bobbed his head back and forth with a Cheshire grin upon his lips. His grip on my hand was firm and purposeful. His other hand soon came in to clutch my hand on the other side, and he began to run his fingertips over my gripped hand, around each knuckle and crease.

From the wrist to the tip of each finger, he seemed to read the array of wrinkles and lines. My hand was a topographical map of interest to this young explorer. It was as if he was using Braille to picture in his mind's eye what this hand really looked like. As he traced each and every detail, he barraged me with one question after another seeking truth and insight.

"What is your last name? Are you married? Do you have kids? What are their names? How old are they? How old are you? Do you have any pets? What are their names? Do you like to hunt? Do you live here?" and on and on and on. Questions that I'm not sure I've even answered for some of my closest friends, but certainly not questions I've answered to a complete stranger. Brian knew more about me in just a few minutes than you would think possible. But did he really care about the answers? Or was he just being inquisitive? Well just a few days later when I ran into him again, I had the answer to my questions.

I saw Brian sitting and eating lunch with another young man. They were talking about their day's activities and things yet to come. I didn't want to disturb them as they were talking, so very politely I just walked up behind Brian and his companion and placed my hand on his shoulder. This action was to give him the understanding that I was there, and perhaps in a moment would like to speak with him, but not to interrupt the conversation he was already having with his friend.

While still speaking with his friend, continuing the story he was already in the middle of, he casually reached up to touch my hand that rested on his shoulder. Without missing a beat, he smiled and matter of factly said, "Hi, Trish." Then as if it were part of the story that he was telling, he began to regale his lunch partner with all the intricate details he had learned about me just a few days earlier. I was amazed. I had not said one word to Brian, yet he knew without a shadow of a doubt that it was me. He told his friend the names of my husband, children, and pets, where I lived, and what I did for a living.

My mouth gaped open in this young man's attempt to acquaint someone to the facts that make up who I am. I began to giggle.

"What's so funny?" Brian asked.

"How did you know it was me I just placed my hand on your shoulder?"

"That's easy," he said. "You have a knobby bump on your middle finger. You're an artist, aren't you? I know because my Mom is, and she has one of those knobby things on her finger, too."

I couldn't speak. I AM an artist, and yes, I DO have a knobby bump on my middle finger from where I hold my pen, brush or pencil. I never told him I liked to paint, draw and write. That wasn't one of his questions. It was something, however, that he knew about me without me having to tell him.

A young man without sight gave me the greatest truth that day. He saw who I really was without ever looking at my face, my clothes, my house, my friends, my job, my accomplishments, my education, or my bank account – things that the world looks at and judges a person by. No, this young man took the time to really see the person he was talking to – things he could hear in my voice and feel through the connection with my hand.

How is it that a person who is blind can have such vision? I don't just casually say hello to someone, ask how they are doing, or walk by without waiting for an answer anymore. I take my time and allow that point of crossing paths with someone to be memorable. A moment that may never happen again which could be a life changing experience for both of us is worth making time for. I don't know if I will ever cross paths with Brian again, but my challenge each day is to SEE what others don't in those I meet.

CHAPTER 4 - BOUNDLESS

What would happen if you took away everything that tied you down? What if you could break the things that shackle you and move totally free? How would that perspective be empowering and allow you to take a totally different outlook on each day you lived? Watching a day in the life of one young man named Luke gave new meaning to being unshackled.

Luke has a condition in which his legs are in braces from the knee down to his shoes, and he uses a walker. Sometimes he is confined to a wheelchair when his legs are too weak to hold him up, even with the help of a walker. He moves with an altered, awkward gait. It pained me to watch him as he tried to keep up with the others and, in the process, tire himself out even more. Even with his limitations, Luke was always smiling and joking around with his friends and bunkmates. It didn't seem to bother him that he didn't stand as tall or as straight as the rest, or that his limitations were more numerous than others around him. He was always about the moment. Living in the moment at hand and getting the most out of it.

I met Luke and his cabin group down at the zip-line course one afternoon. The group was taking turns going up the zip-line pole (a 40-foot telephone pole planted in the ground with a zip-line platform about 27 feet up in the air). They were taking the quick ride down the line with shouts of fear ending in delight. Everyone was either climbing the pole using their own power or with the assistance of a harness and pulley system. It came time for Luke, and his eagerness seemed to charge the air. All of his cabinmates had made the trek, and now it was his turn. He maneuvered his walker and awkwardly made his way over to the base of the tall pole. Knowing he would never be able to traverse the pole on his own, he relented to the cradle harness and allowed himself to be raised to the platform.

Once at the platform, the ropes course crew member manning the platform began her maneuvers to safely place the eager zip-liner in position for his ride. On the ground, Luke could not stand on his own and would teeter back and forth grabbing onto whatever presented itself as a steady support. The zip-line platform was no different, other than it was 27 feet in the air. The staff member struggled to bring Luke onto the platform and get him harnessed to the pole with a safety rope. Then, she unhooked his cradle harness and lowered it to the crew below. She moved swiftly and safely all the while holding onto Luke around the waist. He was most of the time staring at her face to face just inches apart. He would smile really big and tell her, "You are doing a great job." She would smile and thank him, and he would continue to repeat it, thus making the moments lighter and slightly silly. Giggling would begin not only on the platform, but in the group below as Luke made the most of a tense and difficult moment.

Then came the time to hook the zip-line to the harness that was encircling Luke's body. He was too far away, and the staff member was in between him and the zip-line. To move meant having him out in front of her without her being able to help him to the edge of the platform. He would have to walk it, and that was not something he was readily able to do on his own without a walker. Luke could see her situation and the way she was struggling to find a solution. He simply looked at her and lifted his hand to her shoulder. "I got this," he said. "Just give me some room and get behind me. I will do the rest." She smiled knowing that he was right and slowly moved her body to be behind his, all the while holding him around the waist. She leaned forward from behind him and hooked the zip-line to his harness.

"I need you to sit down," she said. "You have to go off the platform sitting, so it won't be such a jolt for you."

"That's not going to happen," he replied. "I'm going to have to go off standing. If I try to sit, I'll fall. I'm pretty sure of that." He smiled and just winked, so she would know that going off standing was his choice and he could handle it. There loomed two good steps between him and the end of the platform. His right foot was always dragging the ground, being the factor that caused him to be off balance and teeter most of the time. It was hardly strong enough to support him if he took a step with his more dependable left side. So now had come the moment of truth. His time to take to the air. He raised his right leg as high as it would go, stepped, pressing the right foot flat, pushed off with his stronger left foot, and took flight. The sheer joy on his face as his arms stretched out wide and as he yelled, "Yeah, baby!" made everyone on the ground cheer and laugh. He was in the moment. He was free.

It was one of the coolest moments that I'd ever experienced, watching a person who lives tethered to the ground and bound by the immobility of their limbs finally break those chains and soar. When I approached Luke, his friends were around him and congratulating him. I told him how awesome that whole experience was to watch. He smiled and said, "You should have lived it. I always wondered what it would be like to walk, really walk like everyone else. Now, that doesn't seem so important, since I know what it feels like to fly."

What a solid truth. We get so bogged down sometimes with the things we see or are experiencing at the moment, that we lose sight of what could be. If we are always looking down, we never see the possibilities up before us, out in front, all around us. This young man had been fine in his day to day living, to that point, smiling as each day went along. But deep down he wondered what it would be like to do something else. Then a new possibility came along, something so out of this world he hadn't even thought to imagine it. Luke taught me that life holds many possibilities, and all of them will provide me with new experiences and new relationships. It is only up to me to try. I can't change anything if I am not willing to try. And when we throw off the things that tether us, we can do the impossible, we are BOUNDLESS.

Trish Wilson

CHAPTER 5 - THE BUTTERFLY EFFECT

The "Butterfly Effect" is the theory that the movement of air produced with every wingbeat of a butterfly makes a wave effect around the world. A small cause making a larger impact. Thus, the hypothesis is that everything we do in life has an effect out in the world. Nothing we do is stagnant. All actions cause another action or reaction from someone or something else. For instance, a small child hosts a lemonade stand in his neighborhood, but instead of raising money for his own pleasure, he is raising the money to help his friend, who suffers from a rare form of Leukemia and needs an expensive treatment. A small action that can cause a great reaction and effect. This butterfly effect happened one day when I met a young woman who never knew the impact she would make.

Nina lives in a silent world of darkness. Not able to hear or see, her vocabulary limited to guttural noises and communication limited to sign language within the palm of her hand, Nina's life is anything but easy. Totally dependent on those around her, she gropes in our world looking for something to hold on to. Nina came to camp for a week of fun with girls her own age. Her cabin leaders knew how to communicate with her and taught those cabinmates her own age a few gestures and sign language letters to be able to communicate with her as well.

She went through her week without much difficulty, enjoying the moments as they came. She painted in arts and crafts, rode a horse for the first time, and enjoyed the swimming pool as well. But the real excitement came the day she went to the ropes course. The girls in her cabin were given the opportunity to decide whether they wanted to travel quickly down the fun zip-line, whose platform sat about 27-feet in the air or choose the very difficult and hotter task of scaling the 30-foot climbing wall. With each of the girls having differing disabilities, each one weighed the choices and all, except one chose to take the fun and easy ride of the zip-line. Each girl was harnessed, and a helmet placed on her head, and each took her place at the foot of the zip-line pole and rose to the platform. When each one zipped off the platform, Nina was given the play by play in her hand via sign language from a counselor. She smiled and gave a guttural cheer of approval, as each girl flew down the line in victory conquering the tall adventurous obstacle.

Then came the moment of truth. It was Nina's turn. The ropes crew chief approached her - a young woman who had been a part of the adventure course for the past three years, and who had finally achieved the position as activity director. She had been struggling personally with the fact that everyone talked about that one camper who gets into your heart and just doesn't leave. Sure, she had past experiences with campers in the previous summers that were memorable, but not that one, the one who would steal her heart. She wanted so badly to have a moment with a camper that would change both of their lives for the better. She just hadn't found the one, yet. As she approached Nina, she checked her harness and began as she had with all the other campers previously, giving her the description of her two choices. Did she want to do the fun, quick, easy zip-line or take the hard, hotter route and struggle up the 30-foot climbing wall? As her attending counselor signed the two options given by the crew chief in her palm, the young Nina smiled and simply signed back one word, W-A-L-L.

The crew chief knew for certain something was lost in the translation and that she misunderstood. Surely no one on such a hot day wanted to fight the battle of struggling up a completely vertical 30-foot monster. Asking the counselor to sign the options one more time, emphasizing the difficulty of the wall option, the crew chief waited for the only answer that could possibly be right, the zip-line. Yet, the answer she just knew the cheerful Nina would give never came. Instead the simple word was again signed out where everyone could see, W-A-L-L. With resignation, the crew chief began rigging up the young persistent camper with the belaying ropes needed to help her on her quest up the 30-foot obstacle.

As Nina approached the face of the wall, the adventure crew realized that she would not be able to hear commands given from the ground as she climbed. So, the crew chief decided to climb with Nina. As they started their first few moves, Nina just stood still as the crew chief placed first her right hand and then her right foot on the holds that would start her on the next level of climbing. Then it became abundantly clear that the crew chief could only operate on one side of the climber. So, both were again lowered to the ground, and the crew chief hooked up a movable roping system for herself, to be able to swing from side to side and aid Nina as she climbed all the way to the top. The adventure began again. A silent ballet of a single girl having her hands and feet moved by a guardian butterfly as she moved swiftly and fluidly behind her. Every time the crew chief would light on Nina's side and place her hand on the young climber's hand a slight giggle would come. Nina was unable to see her assistant, but every time there was a need to move higher, her little butterfly would come and touch her, help her and flutter away. Giggles were the only thank you she could give at the time.

The struggle to the top was apparent as the crew chief climbed twice as much and twice as fast to bring victory to this determined climber. As they approached the top and the young climber had no more wall to face, she had only her hands resting on the top of the wall itself. The crew chief latched her arm around the back of the wall and raised her other arm in victory, screaming, "We did it!" Not wanting to be the bearer of bad news, I pointed and said, "Not yet, she hasn't rung the bell." A single cow bell hangs just above the top of the wall. Each time a camper conquers the wall, they ring that bell to announce across the campus that another warrior has defeated the ominous wall. The crew chief recognizing her oversight, that the young climber couldn't see the bell to know she needed to ring it, reached down and grabbed Nina's closest hand and tapped the bell.

A miracle happened. This young woman knew what was at the end of her daring climb. She had been told on the ground that when she finished climbing, there would be a bell at the top of the wall that she could ring. It would tell everyone the great thing she had accomplished. It would herald to anyone who could hear that she had beaten the wall! When Nina felt the vibration of that first tap of the bell, she knew exactly where she was and exactly what she had just done. She reached back and wacked that cowbell repeatedly, all the while bringing a deep guttural sound that started out low and soft at first building to a shrill of pure joy. She was celebrating 30-feet in the air knowing there were cheers and applause from all of her friends and cabinmates below.

It was at that moment, when Nina was celebrating, that the crew chief realized what she had just witnessed.

Nina was her camper, the one who had entered her heart and changed her life forever. When they both finally came back down to earth and ropes and harnesses were removed, Nina groped around the group of people until she found the crew chief. She reached out and grabbed her hand and signed very softly, "No more walls. I have no more walls in my life, because of you. Thank you, you are my butterfly."

In our lives, we forget that the smallest opportunities can present such amazing results. Nothing is more beautiful than a moment in two lives that changes both forever. The flutter of a butterfly's wings, a very small action, can bring about a tremendous effect. One girl's willingness to do something seemingly impossible, changed her life and the life of the woman who would help her. One woman's willingness to do whatever it took to make an impossible obstacle possible to conquer for another, empowered that young girl to believe she can now do anything. Nina went home and tried more things and showed more people, who and what she was capable of being and doing even with numerous limitations. The crew chief went on to college and received a specialized degree that prepared her for a career working with individuals with physical disabilities and special medical needs in extreme sports and activities. One flutter made a huge EFFECT, not just in one life, but in the many they would interact with in the future.

CHAPTER 6 - SOAR LIKE AN EAGLE

Protecting a child from everything in the world that might harm them, bring them grief, defeat them or cause them pain is not only a tremendous undertaking for parents, it is impossible. There will always be times when children are hurt, suffer pain, are disappointed, lose, or just not get what they think they deserve. And it will be okay. Sure, they will suffer for a brief time, but they will also learn from the experience and grow stronger because of it. But there is also a flip side to this predicament. Some parents believe in brutal honesty which can cause their children to not hope, not dream and not believe that different results can happen if only they try. Telling children, the stark truth often allows no room for possibilities, just grim realities.

I met such a mom one afternoon when she was brought unknowingly to the camp where I worked. Michelle, her husband, and Rudy, their son with disabilities were brought to Kerrville to visit a museum of cowboy art. Rudy loved cowboy art, and his school principal thought it would be great for him to see the collection housed in this special museum. The principal made arrangements for Rudy and his parents to go on this fieldtrip, hoping that he could also show them this special camp that would be fantastic for their son as well. He knew that Michelle was not going to relent simply by describing it to her, but if she saw it for herself there might be a chance.

The principal, an avid supporter of the camp, told the family that on their way back home, he needed to stop and drop something off to someone who worked at the camp close by. That someone was me. When he arrived in the parking lot, I happened to be waiting and approached the specialized vehicle to say hello. Greetings and introductions were given, though somewhat distant and cold on the mother's part, who was seemingly upset at the inconvenience of making the stop. But Rudy, who was the center of attention that day, was warm and eager to meet a new friend. He asked questions, like "What is this place?" and "Do you work here?" I took the time to answer his questions and then offered to show everyone around if they had just a few extra minutes. Everyone, bar one, were more than excited to see the gorgeous campus filled with activity areas and opportunities for children just like Rudy.

Nearly everywhere we went, the equestrian center, the sports lake and archery pavilion, the campsites, and the cabin area, could be seen from the vehicle. But a walking tour was the only way to see the swimming pool and dining facilities. Rudy wanted to see them, and so did his dad. But his mother, well that was a whole other story. Michelle sat crossed-armed in the back of the SUV and had a grimace on her face that would make my mom say, "Your face is going to freeze that way if you don't stop looking like that." She wasn't having any of it. She wanted to be anywhere but where she was, and everyone knew it. Rudy's father exited the vehicle, and with the help of the principal, they unloaded Rudy's wheelchair. After speaking with her husband, Michelle finally exited the vehicle as well, still with arms crossed.

We looked in activity buildings, the dining hall and one of the cabins, ending up at the edge of a beachfront, junior Olympic-sized swimming pool. Rudy smiled and began wheeling around the facility with his father close at hand. They chattered and laughed about all the amazing things they had seen that were perfect for a kid just like him. Michelle was standing, still cross-armed and watching with apprehension while her fragile child circled such a dangerous area, in her opinion. I approached and broke the silence with a question.

"Have you ever seen an eagle."

"No, not up close," she replied obviously annoyed at the question. "Why?"

"They build their nests in the highest places they can find. The top areas of high cliffs and the tops of massively tall trees," I began. Not impressed, and with a "get to the point already" look in her eyes, I moved on. "They build their nests high up to protect their young from predators and to allow their children the drop they need when they get ready to fly." This got her attention. I continued, "Eagle mothers are not unlike us. They provide for their family and protect their children relentlessly. They build a nest and keep their children warm, fed and safe. But then the day comes for flying, when the baby is ready to leave the nest and try its wings for the first time. There is not an eagle mother that probably doesn't hold her breath as she watches that little eaglet fall from the nest the first time."

Her face was totally fixed on mine. I knew that I was explaining in words what she was feeling inside. Her fears for her child were real. She spent every moment of every day caring for him, making things comfortable for him, and protecting him. She had told him honestly that because of his condition and all his special needs, he would never go to college, never date or get married and never be able to have a job. In her mind, she wasn't being cruel, but honest. All those things were difficult for kids, but more so for a child who lives in a wheelchair and has so many physical limitations. But what she didn't realize was that in being honest, she took all hope, all dreams and all excitement out of life for him. What could he look forward to? Nothing. The truth hurt, but it was better she told him so that he wouldn't have to risk being hurt more later. What if he failed? Wouldn't that hurt more than the truth now?

I continued with my object lesson. "When the eagle mother sees that child falling, the whole time she is thinking, 'Stick out your wings and flap.' She watches as that eaglet is tumbling and falling through the air getting closer and closer to the ground. But she built her nest high for that reason. She gave her child plenty of room to figure it out. She allowed her child the opportunity to try. She took a risk, and soon, very soon, when he remembered to stick out his wings, it would all be worth it. The eagle mom waits, and then it happens."

"What? What happens?" she demands, as if I am drawing the story out just to torture her.

I smile and wrap up the tale. "The little eagle sticks out his wings and flaps. Just one little flap, but he flaps. The wind catches his wings, and he begins to soar. He flaps more and begins to rise and soar like he had seen his mom do so many times before. He was just like her, strong and majestic, soaring high above the earth below. He looks up and sees his mom standing on the edge of the nest, with her arms outstretched crowing to the heavens, 'That's my child!'"

She was no longer cross-armed. She had turned and was looking at her son across a large pool of water as he laughed and talked about all he could do at a place like this. I approached her slowly and just leaned in close and asked, "Don't you want that for your child? To see him soar just one time? It's a risk, but what a result if you just will allow him the opportunity. What do you say?" She didn't respond. Her son and husband came back to where we were standing, and their smiles spoke volumes. The group thanked me for my time and said they would discuss the possibility of Rudy attending camp the upcoming summer. When they left, Michelle smiled and waved good bye. No longer were her arms crossed, she was thinking and that was good enough for me.

Rudy came to camp. He rocked camp. Everyone knew his name. He made hundreds of new best friends. He also found the radio activity, where campers can become radio disc jockeys for the day. He loved it and could do it from the confinement of his wheelchair. His body might not work the way he wanted, but his mind and voice were anything but limited. He rode a horse, went camping, played instruments in music, rode in a pedal boat, and lounged in the swimming pool. He had a week he would never forget. He also met kids just like him and realized that there were a lot of things that he could do that he had never tried before. He loved it. He soared.

At the end of the week, parents and guests are invited to attend the awards ceremony as the culmination of the accomplishments by the campers during the week. Rudy's family attended. His parents, his younger sister, and his twin brother all attended. I never realized that he had siblings, much less an identical twin, well almost identical. His twin was completely able bodied. A healthy, athletic young man who looked like his brother in almost every way, minus the cerebral palsy and wheelchair. They sat and watched the festivities as the campers entered the amphitheater, and the party began. Cheers, songs, and presentations were made, awards announced and given. The best at swimming, the best at archery, and the best at radio – guess who won that award. You guessed right. A surprised but proud family screamed and clapped as their young camper accepted his certificate.

The last awards go to the outstanding campers for the week. These young people exemplify the "CAN DO" mindset. They try everything, have a positive attitude and encourage all those around them to do their best as well. When this award went to my young friend, I was screaming loud. The entire amphitheater erupted. Every camper cheered his name as he wheeled down to receive this top award. I stopped for just a moment and turned my attention from the overjoyed young man to see his family, especially his mother. There she was standing with her husband and other children. But unlike them, Michelle wasn't clapping, or cheering. She was standing, arms outstretched, tears streaming down her face. She was unable to say anything or do anything else. The smile on her face spoke volumes. She knew the risk was great, but she took it. In taking that risk, she afforded her child the opportunity to risk as well. Risk trying new things – and finding radio. Risk meeting new people – and finding lifelong friends. Risk leaving her for a week – and finding a life that would carry him well into his future, to share with his mom and bring her joy.

After the ceremony, I met up with the newly energized family. The parents were more than ecstatic, and the sister was happy to see her brother again. But the twin brother was the surprise. He was so impressed with his brother. He realized how cool his brother really was. He said, "I always thought of my brother as fragile and unable to do so many things. I never realized that he had so much inside of him. I am pumped about spending more time with him and really getting to know all he can do." Michelle came over and put her arm around me and said, "Thank you." She left with her family, and as they left, her young eagle was still talking about his experience and all the things that he had planned once they got home.

Since that time, Rudy has graduated from online college, has a steady girlfriend and worked at his local radio station through high school and college. His family has grown closer. They are no longer a family of just stark reality, but of possibilities and dreams. This experience taught me the harsh reality that fear robs us of the possibilities in life. When we allow fear to rule our minds, our hearts and our spirit, we stop hoping, imagining and dreaming. Risks are scary, but not taking risks is scarier. The what if's in life haunt those who never step outside their comfort zone. Give yourself an opportunity to do the things that you've only dreamed of doing. Don't allow your fears to stand in the way of your future or those around you. Allow yourself the opportunity to fail, to tumble and even to fall. Then maybe, just maybe, you'll remember who you are, what you were created to do and stretch out your wings and catch the air, and finally, you'll end up SOARING like an eagle!

Trish Wilson

CHAPTER 7 - LIVING ON PURPOSE

Each of us is designed for a specific purpose, something that we are to do that no one else can or will do. There is a uniqueness about each of us, and that uniqueness, or purpose should drive us every day. Mark Twain said it best, "The two most important days in your life are the day you are born and the day you find out why." Everyone struggles to find that purpose, the reason why they are here. When you realize that each day is an opportunity to live in that purpose, walk in that purpose and act in that purpose – your days start to have a different meaning. You'll see that purpose unveil itself throughout your life.

Marley was one of those unique characters who finds her purpose early in life. Though a young teenager, she had something that was out there just for her, and she found it after a week of serving others. Marley had a servant's heart. She looked for opportunities to help those around her who not only needed it, but also those who didn't know they needed it. She stepped into situations without thinking, "What's in this for me." She just wanted to help.

She didn't fit the physical look of those around her at camp. She didn't traverse in a wheelchair or with a walker. She didn't have braces on her legs or prosthetics attached to her body. She didn't look like she had a special medical condition at all. But she did. She was born with a problem in her brain. She had life-saving brain surgery shortly after birth that helped her to live a normal life. Her parents hesitated to send her to camp, afraid that there was another child, more physically stricken than their daughter, who should take her place. But Marley wanted to go, and she needed to go. If there were questions or hesitations about her participation, all of them were squelched the first moment she arrived on campus.

She fit right in. She came expecting a fun week of thrilling activities and found that and more. She had an unselfish giving nature – basically a servant's heart. A rare quality found in the youth of today. In her cabin, she met other young women who each had different disabilities. One, in particular, had an issue with seizures. Staying calm and maintaining a regular rhythm throughout the day helped to keep her seizures to a minimum. Marley looked at this cabinmate and saw an opportunity to help. She befriended the young woman and in a calm nature introduced herself and explained the things that she had found out about their fun week ahead. The entire week, you never saw the two separated. Marley made sure to maintain a calm and quiet nature during each activity throughout the week, and together they enjoyed every moment - calm, cool and collected. The smiles on their faces spoke volumes. Both were changed forever by the other. Marley was always helping others as well, but not like the attention she gave her new special friend. At the end of the week, tears streamed as they both said their good-byes and went their separate ways. Marley, turning and reuniting with her family, seemed different somehow. They began to load her luggage into the car when she announced that she knew what she wanted to do with her life. Both of her parents had heard her talking about nursing in times past, but her tone was different this time. "What is that, sweetie?" her mother asked in a very interested manner. "A pediatric neurosurgeon!" she announced.

The shock on her parent's faces said it all. "What? Are you serious? You've always talked about being a nurse," her dad reminded her. "I know," she replied. "But I want to do even more. I figured that I could help more children like me and my new friend if I were a surgeon." Her parents were surprised, but proud. Their daughter had not only had a great week, but found her purpose in the process. She would be able to use her true nature, as a servant, to do great things in her future. What a dynamic young woman, who had just begun the next phase in her quest for fulfilling her PURPOSE in life.

Trish Wilson

CHAPTER 8 - LIFE IS A STAGE

In an old Shakespearean play, one of the characters states, "All the world's a stage, and all the men and women merely players." The quote is not too far off, except the concept is too small. Life is a stage. And the time we are a part of it is our time to shine. Your time could be a drama, or a comedy, or heaven forbid a tragedy, or a combination of all of them. Whatever your life, it is on display for others to see, experience, and hopefully enjoy.

I've been fortunate to have seen some of the best Broadway shows in their prime – <u>The King and I</u>, <u>Sound of Music</u>, and <u>Cats</u> - and concerts with artists that I will never forget. But I really enjoy productions that have dancing, probably because I wish I could dance like those carefree talented people on the stage. (My klutzy nature prevents the graceful moves.) Among the countless hours of enjoyment from those who entertained and enriched my life, I can pick a 5-minute performance one summer day, as the most memorable - when a young girl performed the most beautiful dance

I'd ever seen. To this day, I can see her dance and smile and hear the song just as I did that day.

When I first saw Paula at the camp, she was running and playing with friends. She looked like every other child you'd see, except for the two prosthetic legs she had from the knee down. They were bright pink with big white daisies on them. I thought they were just socks on her legs, until closer examination. Paula moved just as quickly and just as easily as the others she was playing with.

All week I watched Paula run and move with ease. Her man-made appendages did exactly what they were created to do in aiding her movement. She was a beautiful girl with big placid blue eyes and straight blonde hair like Marsha Brady. She had a smile that would melt your heart. Other than having two prosthetic legs, you'd say there was nothing physically wrong. Paula sang and whistled and laughed wherever she went and made sure others were doing the same.

At the talent show at the end of the week, I saw Paula had signed up. I knew that she would be singing and probably lead a sing-along with the entire audience to share her time on stage. I stood in the very front, close to the stage to get pictures of the children as they performed. While standing there, I saw Paula back stage in the wing curtains off to the side. She looked nervous, tugging at her clothes, shuffling back and forth on her hot pink legs and tennis-shoed feet. A young boy was finishing his talented act of burping the names of all his cabinmates and receiving thunderous applause and cheers. Then it was Paula's turn.

As the young artist before her exited the stage, she simply sat down in the wings and began to remove her prosthetic limbs. I wondered what she was doing. I knew she would be singing for her talent, and surely, she could sing with her prosthetic legs still on her body. But then she stood up on her stumps, the stage grew dark and the music began. Paula leapt out onto the stage. Her stumps thudded with each hit on the hard-wooden floor. I cringed a bit, thinking, "OUCH! That must hurt!" But you'd never guess that it did by looking at this young performer's face. She smoothly flowed from one graceful position to another, linking her movements into a dance that would rival any on the "World's" stage.

She synced her movements with the beat of the music and truly proved that "Girls just want to have fun." It was incredible. I stood and watched in awe as this young dancer with no feet showed that the impossible could be possible, if just given the opportunity. The music began to come to an end, and a grand finale leap and spin brought the entire audience to a deafening applause. As the music died, Paula stood in the spotlight with her arms extended and a smile that wrapped around to the back of her head, all the while drinking in the last glorious moments of her ovation. She was living her dream and didn't want to miss a second of it. This was her moment.

As she left the stage, shimmying on her little stumps, she grabbed her prosthetics and moved quickly to a ramp and ended up by my feet in front of the stage. She meticulously re-attached her legs, and I watched still speechless from what I had just witnessed. I knelt beside her and asked, "May I ask you a question?" She stopped and smiled saying, "You want to know why I took off my legs." "Yes, I do," I replied. She very sweetly looked me in the eye and said, "Sometimes you have to take off what the world gives you to be what you were created to be. I'm a dancer. I just needed a stage to prove it."

I was dumbfounded. How can one so young be so smart? How can a child with so much to be frustrated, angry, upset, and possibly sad about be so well grounded? She knows who she is – and more importantly, she knows what she can do. How much have we weighed ourselves down with what the world tells us we are, or what we can, or in most cases, what we can't do? Isn't it time that we take off what the world has given us and be who we were created to be? We are each unique. We can't let others define us. There is beautiful music in each day of our lives. The stage is ready - get out there and DANCE!

CHAPTER 9 - UP AGAINST THE WALL

Limitations can be viewed through two different lenses. First, limitations are those things which impede our progress, or success. The things that hold us down to the life we just live because we can't do anything else. Or, limitations can compel us to reach beyond what we know, feel or see to the unknown, to a place we've only imagined. It is only an act of will that is needed, a simple choice that will provide a different outcome. A moment of truth, a moment that hangs between these two options – an obstacle or opportunity. Witnessing such a moment in a life, when the decision to be made is made. Observing the transformation of a life and a body with so many limitations to a life with a new outlook, new focus, new purpose is a moment you will never forget.

When Donny viewed the 30-foot climbing wall from the seat of his daily companion, his wheelchair, it looked much taller than it really was. Holds, strategically placed up the ominous beast, presented opportunity for any climber ready for the challenge. But, how could he even begin to climb with all his limitations? Born without legs and one of his arms, he came to the task of climbing without all the necessary physical tools. But, his determination to reach the top outweighed the voices within telling him, "Impossible."

As the adventure course crew placed gear on his fragile body, his mind pushed into overdrive, strategizing a possible solution to the impossible task before him. "Are you ready? Do you have a plan?" the crew chief asked. Donny asked, "Can you give me a minute?" He sat in his protective climbing gear, looking at the formidable foe, and wondered, "How in the world am I going to do this?" The activity crew waited for his plan, not offering a plan of their own, allowing the young man to struggle for a solution on his own, as he would have to do the rest of his life without their assistance. Calling on his own strength, his own determination, would get him through this challenge and all the others he would face throughout the days ahead. The crew waited patiently. Then it happened. Like a flash of a bright light, the smile appeared on Donny's face, and he had his plan for success. Though difficult and not the obvious way to climb, a possible solution to the impossible task was his.

The crew stood ready for his instructions, spotters around his chair ready to help him start and to catch him if he faltered. The crew member held on to the belaying rope that was attached to his harness to steady him and reduce the slack in his rope as he climbed. His cabinmates stood as observers of the adventure waiting for their friend. If Donny climbed and built up slack in his rope, his belayer would pull the rope taut, preventing any struggle with his overall body weight. Plus, if he slipped or lost his grip for a second, the belayer would help to hold him in position on the wall, safely allowing him to refocus and regain his momentum. The only thing that the belayer could not and would not do is pull the climber up the wall. That feat was all up to the climber. Building the slack was the only step to progress.

As the crew readied themselves, Donny asked if his wheelchair could be pushed as close to the wall as possible. The crew obliged, and Donny now sat eye-to-eye with a "hold" on the wall. He reached out and gripped it with his only hand, as if to say, "Glad to meet you. Now I'm going to conquer you." He twisted his head to everyone around him and charged, "Let's do this!" And it began. He pulled his limited frame up and placed his chin on the top of the hold his hand had been gripping, keeping his body balanced as he reached above his head for the next hold. As he reached his arm up, he moved it back and forth running his hand along the surface of the wall searching for the next hold. Slowly, he would find a hold, then another, and another – placing his chin in each, as he built slack in his line. With every move upward, more slack would build in the rope and the belayer would pull the rope taut. His cabinmates came to his aid, yelling directions for his arm to move to find the next hold. Working as a team, the crew watching his ascent with safety and well-being their focus, the cabinmates yelling helpful directions with encouragement their focus, and the young climber fighting with each movement with success his focus, the dynamic moment unfolded as a pivotal point in Donny's life.

Sweating and struggling, he continued to fight, strive, reach and find his way up the vertical barrier standing between him and the goal he set before he started. Each hold, each grip of his single hand and pull of his strong arm, each balance of his frame on the point of his chin, each movement sapped energy out of the young climber's body, but energized his resolve. Others, watching and wondering, cheered him on and stood in amazement as the top of the wall became more within reach. A lone cowbell hung from a cord just above the edge of the wall, waiting for the next victor to come along. As Donny, tired and worn out, reached the last hold and extended his arm up and past the top of the wall to swat only air. He knew he had reached his goal. He pushed up and placed his chin on the very top of the wall. Face-to-face with the bell, a wry smile danced upon his lips. He released his grip on the wall and, hanging only by his chin, hit the bell and allowed it to herald his victory. He leaned his body back and away from the wall, allowing the belayer to lower him effortlessly to his wheelchair. His joy was apparent, and the crowd of his friends and the adventure crew below celebrated his amazing outcome as he victoriously returned to earth. As he stripped off his climbing gear and received single-handed "high-fives," he smiled and exclaimed, "Now, tell me what a one-armed man can't do!"

What some see as limitations, others see as challenges. Our choice to limit determines our outcome even before we begin. But to see limitations in our lives as challenges or tools for a bigger challenge, makes the possibilities limitless. Not having two hands, two arms, two feet and two legs and thinking about climbing a 30-foot wall might seem a little crazy. But how awesome to see not your limitations, but your abilities, and think of a different method to achieving the goal and reaching the top. When you find yourself up against the walls, barriers, or obstacles of life, they no longer have to be impossible. You can see them as opportunities to use what you have and who you are to do the amazing. What is going to be your focus? Limitations or possibilities? Each day the choice is yours. Don't let the obstacles in life intimidate you. See them for what they are – opportunities. Live LIMITLESS!

CHAPTER 10 – A MILE IN MY SHOES

The saying goes, "You don't really know what someone is dealing with until you walk a mile in his shoes." That is so true. When someone says, "I know what you are going through," or "I know how you feel," do they really know? Have they really walked a mile in my shoes? Sometimes when people don't know what to say, they say things like that. But, very few of us have been in someone's exact plight or situation. Until you have gone through exactly what someone else has gone through, with all the same dynamics, you really don't have any idea of what they should or should not feel, or what they should or should not do, or how they should or should not react. That's what happened to me.

About five years ago, I went to work one Thursday, and was sitting at my desk working on projects that were prioritized by importance, when I started feeling a little light-headed and dizzy. I pulled back from my desk and just closed my eyes for a moment to change my perspective and give myself a little time to recoup. Then, as though the floor in my office disappeared, I felt as though I was spinning and falling from the sky without a parachute. I grabbed my desk and laid my head down on the cool surface to find an anchor, something that would make the falling cease. Stability did not come. It didn't matter that I was holding on to a desk or sitting in a chair, the uneasy and rapid feeling of falling continued. I couldn't open my eyes without the room spinning around sideways and from the top to the bottom as well. But closing my eyes wasn't much help either. I was quickly approaching a sense of nausea that I could not liken to anything I had ever experienced before. I couldn't do anything, couldn't move without feeling more out of control.

I reached for my cell phone and called my doctor. He prescribed some antibiotics for an inner ear infection and suggested for me to go home and rest. Before I could call my husband to see if he could come and get me, the feeling of being out of control grew worse. My senses now had me spinning diagonally as well. I couldn't stop spinning, my vision grew more blurred, and my fear grew to sheer terror. I hit the intercom on my desk phone and cried for my boss. He came quickly to my office and to his surprise found me clutching my desk with a Vulcan death grip. He carried me to his office where he had a couch for me to rest on and called my husband to come and retrieve me. I held onto the couch with all my strength continuing to feel as though the amusement parks really needed to mimic this ride for others to experience. However, there was no fun to this ride for me, just panic and a feeling of falling forever.

Once home, the medicines didn't seem to help at all. If anything, the spinning grew worse. With each passing day, I kept thinking, "Just give the medicine time to work." But, two days in, I was unable to sleep, had not been able to keep food or water down, and the dizziness was not easing. I woke up on the third day unable to move. I could not get my legs or arms to move the way I wanted them to. I couldn't even get my head to pull up off the pillow. It felt like a 100-pound weight. I didn't know what was wrong and didn't know what to do. Gratefully, my doctor is a friend. My husband called him and described in a concerned tone the problems I was having. The doctor told him to bring me into his office right away, and he'd meet us there. My husband dressed me and carried me to the car, since I was unable to do anything to assist. Once at the office, my doctor met us in the parking lot. He was concerned at my condition and how fast I had deteriorated. He told my husband to take me across the street to the hospital. I was admitted, in a room, and hooked to an IV in less than 10 minutes. A specialist came in to my room to begin running some tests, which caused me to throw up on his shoes. I was rushed to an MRI and CAT scan to see what else could be the problem, and to rule out a stroke. I had no idea of why I couldn't move, just that I was scared and had to rely completely on others for my care.

I'm independent. Anyone who meets me would say that statement is true. I'm strong, strong-willed, motivated, creative, out-going and did I say, independent? Well, now you get the picture. Having others take care of everything for me, about me, really didn't set well with me. I can do it, or at least, I was able to do it just a few days ago. On the third night in the hospital, I was low. I was down and depressed, unable to see the reason behind something like this happening to me. I had things to do. People counted on me. I had responsibilities that weren't being taken care of because I was sick. I was sick, really sick, and no one knew why. I was angry, upset, disappointed and hurting emotionally. Spiritually I realized that for the first time in my life, God had blown it. He had made a mistake. He allowed this weird problem to be a part of my life. Surely, he knew that he had made a mistake. If he didn't know, I was there to tell him. I began to cry out in my dark hospital room. My cries turned into sobs. Sobs turned into railings of anger, and then just to quiet desperate whimpers. WHY was the repetitive word. Why would God let this happen? Why was this happening to ME? Why now, when I have so much I need to do? Why take away the very things I need to do the job, the ministry that He gave me to do? Why can the doctors not find the cause? Why can't they find the right treatment? Why am I in so much pain? Why am I so scared? Why do I feel like He isn't here? Why? Why? Why?

In the quiet dark, I looked for answers and found only silence. I didn't find anything that would satisfy my mind, but I did find something that would calm my heart. In the stillness, I felt a peace and heard a voice say, "I am and will always be in all of your why's. This is about much more than why it happened. It is about what you will learn as you go through it. Wait. Be still. Watch. Know." I knew that up and to this point, God had been the rudder to my boat, the wind in my sail and the rock on which I stand. Now, more than ever, I must realize that my reliance on myself is faulty. But my reliance on God is the only solid ground I could ever stand on. Either I believe that His plan, including the rough patches, is greater and better than mine, or I don't. I chose at that moment to believe in His plan, even if I didn't know all the why's and to look for what I would learn instead. I always seem to get bogged down in the details and forget that He's got those already. I just need to stay focused on the big picture – HIM! I slept for the first time in almost a week. It was a peaceful sleep. It was like the song says, "Sleep in heavenly peace."

The next day, I had a visitor. Zac and his family are friends of mine, and fortunately he qualified to attend camp as well. I call every child that I meet, who becomes a part of my heart and life, my un-child. I may not have birthed them into this world, but I would gladly have them as one of my own. Zac is one of my favorite un-children. He came with his family to visit me in the hospital. He knew that I was terribly sick and asked if he could visit me. As this young boy entered the room as any young boy would, running like a bull in a china closet, I cringed as he bee-lined for my bed, afraid he would hit it. I waited for the impact and the immediate tailspin my head would enter. Yet, he stopped just shy of the bed, slowed to a walk, and placed his hand gently on the covers near my knee. "I came to see you," he said with an impish smile. "Thank you for coming," I said as I struggled to move my chin down so that I could see him more clearly. Realizing that I couldn't see him, he began to move a chair in the corner to the foot of the bed. He ascended his unsteady perch and peered down at me like a giant. Smiling a snaggle-toothed smile, he announced, "Now, you can see me! And I can see you better, too!" His parents entered the room just a few seconds later, out of breath after chasing after their son, who had run ahead of them, as always. I conversed with his parents awhile, telling of the testing and search for cause and treatment. They gave their words of encouragement and assurance of continued prayers on my behalf.

"Can we pray for her now?" Zac asked. "Yes, we can," his mother answered. "Okay, then I will pray," he replied. A sweet action on his part, would forever change my view on angels who walk among us. Zac removed the covers from my feet and placed his sweet fingers around the big toes like a tiny crab. He lifted his face to the ceiling and began to pray. As if this young soul had been in my room the night before, he spoke from God's heart to mine.

"God, thank you for being here in the hospital with us. Thank you for Ms. Trish. Help her to know that everything is going to be okay. Help her not be scared. Help her to know that sometimes the doctors have to hurt us to help us. And make her better real fast, so she can be at camp when I am there. I love her. I love you. Amen." Zac jumped off the chair and asked if he could go ride the elevator again and bolted out of the room. He left as quickly as he came. "I appreciate you bringing him to see me today before school. I know that things are busy with school having just started," I said to Zac's mother. "Oh. No, we aren't on our way to school. We are on our way to his next operation in Dallas. We just had to stop here before we left town. He insisted. He knew he wouldn't be able to see you for a while. So, we had to come today, before we left town," she answered with a smile.

Zac has physical challenges of his own. He has a bone fusion problem and must have bones in his body broken and reshaped to allow him to grow as he needs. He has had more operations and procedures in his few years than I will in my lifetime. He definitely knows what it is like to walk a mile in my shoes. He prayed that prayer with sincere empathy. He knows that medical personnel must hurt us to help us sometimes. He knows that it is hard sometimes to feel like God is with us in the hospital, yet knows that He is. He knows that I will get better, because HE KNOWS.

A week into my stay in the hospital, the tests came back negative for everything except a viral labyrinthitis of the vestibular nerve. What that means in a nutshell is a very vital nerve that connects our eyes, ears, and brain to each other and communicates to the rest of our body to tell it what to do, was fried by a virus which attacked it from a sinus infection I unknowingly had. The prognosis was that with high-dose steroids and medicines to make an unhospitable environment for the virus, the nerve might be able to regenerate. The regeneration would be a slow process, and within a year or so, I would be able to regain some of my mobility, hopefully. It was an unsure future, a painful recovery and an unknown outcome, but I was not alone. I had faithful friends and family praying for me, walking with me through recovery. I had awesome doctors and professionals who were skilled and dedicated to helping me achieve. And dynamic examples of faith and perseverance, like Zac, who go through each of their days knowing that it is something special.

Today, I am fully recovered. I am no longer on any medications and live dizzy-free (at least medically). I recovered at a tremendously surprising rate as well. A process that they believed would take a year or more to have all my faculties return, only took about 6 months. I am not an overachiever, well not in this case. I just had a drive of purpose within me. A knowing that there was more to be done each day. That those around me were watching, wanting to see what and who I believed in. There is a purpose for everything in our lives – something to learn, something to do, something to give, something to gain. I saw the struggle to recover as an opportunity to walk in someone else's shoes. I could not do everything on my own. I HAD to rely on the care of others. In doing so, I gained a new appreciation of the heart of service that so many around me have. I am blessed to have had this experience, though difficult and confusing as to why at the time. Walking daily in step with God, makes me more aware of opportunities to WALK in step with others as they journey along their path.

Trish Wilson

PROLOGUE

We do not meet others by accident, coincidence or chance. Each of us are in the life of another to give a blessing or receive a blessing. If we are lucky, both happen at the very same time. When you are given a new day, you have ONE more day, to do ONE more thing, to change ONE more life, even if it is your own. So, don't miss the opportunity. When you live each day like this, you realize that setting out to change someone's life usually will change your life as well. The places you go and the things you do will be more fun. The people you meet will be more fascinating.

I never had trouble meeting people, or talking to people, or using my imagination to create pictures, whether in art or writing. I was seen in our church nursery, as a baby, standing behind a large stack of building blocks, preaching to the other babies who sat drooling and listening to my jabber. I never had trouble making presentations or public speaking throughout my years in grade school, college or seminary. I ministered, through Bible studies and drama to countless groups across the country. I love to write, draw, paint and act, all with scripture and encouraging others as the focus of each piece. I work in a secular job, which allows me to use every gift, talent and skill to speak encouragement to every demographic possible and bring others to the point where they might eventually see that they too have a purpose and strive to discover it. I am here on this planet to build up and encourage others to live their life on purpose, to see each day, as I do, as a building block in that purpose. My day is filled with making a difference in the life of someone using what I have learned and can do as my tools. I look forward to each day knowing that each one is different in scope, but focused in purpose.

You are never too young or too old to discover the purpose for your life. There are so many people out in the world just going through life. They see each day as just another day. They go through life thinking that every day is the same and there is nothing else. But there is. I have learned that my purpose today may be part of the bigger purpose in my life, but it also may be directing me to a new purpose as well. I leave my options open and see each day as a new prospect to discover, grow and create. Watching others around me find their purpose, act in their purpose and live in their purpose makes me smile. I see the joy that they have in the things that they do and the person they have become. If I can have a small part in that purpose, it thrills me.

When we fulfill our purpose to the fullest, then what? Is that it? No, I don't believe so. I believe, if I have a breath in my lungs, a beat of my heart, and another day in front of me – there is purpose for my life, today. The great thing is that I get to search for it and find it like the treasure it is. I might have a different purpose today than I had yesterday, but there is still a reason and a purpose for me right now. When you arise each morning, live today like you mean it. Spend every day living on purpose. Then at the end of your days, you'll look back on your life, see how amazing it was, and smile.

The chapters of this book are about just a few individuals, who over the past 10 years, crossed my path for a specific time with a specific purpose to change a life, mine. They taught me about who I am, who I can be and how to see potential in others. Oh, you might say that more than my life was changed in some of these instances, but I guarantee you, the change in my life was something that I wasn't expecting. The names of the individuals I mentioned in this book have been changed. I did this out of kindness to them, and to allow you to see those in your life that might resemble them. Someone who brings to your life the very characteristic, aspect, attribute, or attitude that they brought to mine.

I pray that this little book will help those who read it to see the purpose in their lives and in each life that crosses their paths as they journey each day. I am thankful for all of those who have crossed my path in these first 50 years. Thank you for leaving your mark and making a difference. I pray that for that ONE moment we were together, I did ONE thing that changed your life for the better. For those I will meet in the days and years ahead, I look forward to meeting you, to sharing with you, to praying with you, to making a difference with you and for you. Here's to our moment together, may it be the ONE we all will never forget!

INTERACTIVE
JOURNALING

Now that you have finished the book, there is an opportunity for reflection. Thoughts of people you have met, who perhaps fit one of those mentioned in the book have flooded your mind and heart over the course of reading. You remembered fondly the one, who reached into your life and changed it for the better, bringing light into your darkness, a smile to your face and joy to your heart.

Hopefully you will continue with the interactive journaling section that follows which will pose questions and points to ponder, answer, and share with others. My greatest hope is that you will be encouraged by this book and in turn you will share it with someone, who has changed your life in some way. Be the ONE for someone today!

Trish Wilson

Intro –

Reflection:
Describe your life as a genre, i.e. Drama, Comedy, etc.

List 3 people who have been a part of your life and made it better. Tell how they made it better.

List 1 person who brought you heartache in the past and what you learned from that relationship that has made you stronger.

Action:
Write a note to someone from your past who made your life better and tell them how much they mean to you.

<u>Chapter 1 – Being Different</u>

Reflection:

What makes you different from anyone else?

Is what others think of you important in what you attempt to do?

What have you not tried doing, because you just don't didn't think you could?

What does the phrase "What you put in, you get out" mean to you?

If you could change the things that make you different, unique, would you? Why?

Who do you know who is different and doesn't let anything stand in their way? What would you say to them if you could say anything?

Action:
Look at another person's differences and think of 3 ways that their differences set them apart for doing the incredible. Send them an encouraging note heralding their amazing uniqueness and potential and what you have learned from them.

Chapter 2 – Worth a Thousand Words

Reflection:

Draw a picture of a smiley face without lifting your pen, like this:

Now draw the same face, but with your eyes closed, like this: (don't laugh too hard!)

Describe in words a time someone made you feel encouraged and smile.

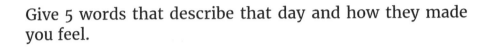

Give 5 words that describe that day and how they made you feel.

Recall a time that you made someone smile. What happened and how did that smile on their face make you feel?

Action:
Smile at everyone you meet and see how many smile back. Report back here what happened.

Leave a smiley face note for 5 people to find somewhere along the way.

Chapter 3 – A Man of Vision

Reflection:

What do people see when they look at you?

What do you want people to see when they look at you?

Draw your life in a picture.

Action:

This week stop when you ask someone how they are doing and wait for their response. Take time to listen to their words, hear the cry of their heart and get to know them.

Trish Wilson

<u>Chapter 4 – Boundless</u>

Reflection:
What inhibits you from doing the impossible?

Put a word on each chain link that is something
that binds you and keeps you from doing the things you
want to.

What have you not done just because you believed it was
too risky? Or that you would get hurt?

What could you do to help someone else succeed at
something they have hesitated in trying?

In chapter 4 it says, "If we are always looking down, we never see the possibilities up before us, out in front and all around us." How is that statement true in your life?

Action:
Encourage someone who is operating outside of their comfort zone or trying to do something they've never done before.

Take a risk and do something you've never done before this week. Plan and then do it! Don't let fear control your life.

Chapter 5 – The Butterfly Effect

Reflection:
In the book it states, "Everything we do in life has an effect out in the world." In knowing this, what actions have you taken today which will affect someone's life today?

What little thing has someone done for you in the past that made a huge impact in your life?

In knowing small opportunities can present amazing results, what small part can you play in someone's life to make it amazing today?

Action:
Notice someone who is doing small things that make a great impact on the lives of others and herald them. Make them a poster, note or sign that congratulates them on being a person of action making an impact in the life of another. Just knowing someone noticed means a lot to many.

Trish Wilson

Chapter 6 – Soar Like an Eagle

Reflection:
What things have you been told that were harsh realities or truths that caused your heart to break?

What has fear prevented you from doing?

In the book it states, "when fear is in charge it stops us from hoping, imagining or dreaming." What hopes, or dreams have been lost or just put on hold because of fear in your life?

What is one of your dreams you will not give up on no matter what anyone tells you?

Action:

Find a picture, poster, sculpture, or any item that has an eagle on it. Put that piece somewhere where you will be able to see it each day and know that you are ready to SOAR! Get another one for a friend as well. Leave one behind when you eat out for your server and write on it – remember you are an eagle and SOAR!

Chapter 7 – Living on Purpose

Reflection:

Why do you think you are here? What is your purpose?

If you have a map or blueprint on how to life your life daily and don't use it – What is your life going to look like at the end? What will still be standing in your life??

Action:

Come up with 4 positive attributes you have, or you would like to have for each letter in your name. Then place those attributes on note pad sheets around you so that you see multiples a day and know how awesome you are. (i.e.; Terrific, Reachable, Intelligent, Special, Honorable, etc.).

Trish Wilson

Chapter 8 – Life is a Stage

Reflection:
You have already decided if your life is a comedy, a drama or a tragedy. What is the one thing you want people to remember about your life?

What were you designed to do on this earth?

What do you want to get rid of that the world has given you, so you can be what you were created to be?

Describe a moment when someone amazed you with what they were able to do, even with their limitations.

Action:

Applaud someone when they do something wonderful or helpful to you. Give them praise verbally, written and even clap for them if the moment warrants it. We don't thank people enough for all they can and will do to be a servant.

Seek out someone who is trying to do something great and join them in it. Whether it is a fundraiser for a local charity, or a service project in your community, seek out areas that you can participate and broaden the stage of your life and your impact.

Chapter 9 – Up Against the Wall

Reflection:
Describe the person who inspires you the most and tell why.

Who is the one person that you have met in your life whose limitations not only never impeded them, they inspired you both. Give their story here.

When you face difficulties, obstacles and you don't
see a way out, who do you turn to for encouragement?
Why?

Write of a time when you encouraged someone else
who was struggling against their wall in life.

Action:

When you see an obstacle in the life of someone else, help them to meet that challenge straight on. Help them to see the obstacle as an opportunity for growth. Be the one who cheers others on when they need it the most.

Send a note or notes to someone who is going through rehabilitation (either physical or substance abuse). Cheer them on in the uphill battle in front of them. Help them to see the things that they have within themselves to face the obstacle in front of them. Help them choose hope and fight to achieve their goals.

Chapter 10 – A Mile in My Shoes

Reflection:

When have you been at a dark moment in your life when you didn't have answers and really didn't know if you ever would? Talk about it here.

What or who was it that helped to brighten your path and lead you out of that darkness into a new hope and light? How did they do it?

What lesson did you learn from that experience about yourself and those who served around you in your time of need?

In the book, there is mentioned that every time we meet someone there is something to gain and to give; receive or discard, to grow or to plant, to share or to take. Tell of a time that you gained from meeting someone and a time when you gave.

If where we are going in life is not by accident and the people we have met along the way are not by coincidence, then in your journey looking back, tell of a time that this principal rang obviously true.

Action:
Today as you meet people, and go throughout your daily schedule, see each moment as a point of contact. When you meet someone, or go somewhere, see the moment and live it fully and be with those that are there completely. Enjoy the possibilities. Report back what amazing things happen.

Prologue –

Reflection:

When you live your life on purpose, each day is a new opportunity to focus on that purpose and move within a beautifully orchestrated piece that is yours alone. Your life is not like anyone else's. You will do the things that only you are to do and meet certain people that no one else will get to know. Knowing all this, what is the one thing you hope will happen today?

In looking back through the book at all the different characters, who in your life has similar characteristics? Who are they and what are their characteristics?

Which character have you been in someone else's life?

Action:

Make notes in the journaling section of this book. Underline your favorite quotes. Make notations in the side bars and even make a dedication in the front of the book and then pass it along. Give it to someone who made a difference in your life.

Think of ONE more thing that you can do today for ONE more person. Remember it doesn't have to be elaborate. Simple works! And then do it! Make a point daily of finding a way to help, do, be whatever needs to be done change a life of someone around you! You will make an impact that will last past your life time and will echo in eternity.

Made in the USA
Middletown, DE
19 January 2019